In the Millennium

In the Millennium

Barry McKinnon

VANCOUVER | NEW STAR BOOKS | 2009

NEW STAR BOOKS LTD.
107 — 3477 Commercial Street
Vancouver, BC V5N 4E8   CANADA

1517 — 1574 Gulf Road
Point Roberts, WA 98281   USA

www.NewStarBooks.com
info@NewStarBooks.com

Publication of this work is made possible by grants from the Canada Council, the Department of Canadian Heritage, the Province of British Columbia, and the British Columbia Arts Council.

Cover design by Mutasis.com
Cover photograph by Joy McKinnon
Printed on 100% post-consumer recyled paper
Printed and bound in Canada by Gauvin Press
First printing, November 2009

LIBRARY AND ARCHIVES CANADA CATALOGUING IN PUBLICATION

McKinnon, Barry, 1944–

  In the millennium / Barry McKinnon.

Sections of this 13-part sequence of poems were published previously under the same title.

ISBN 978-1-55420-047-4

I. Title.
PS8525.K5162 2009   C811'.54   C2009-905062-5

for Joy

Contents

In the Millennium

what is it
we know / or imagine   get to

what thought known   to be ahead
in life, one inch from the beginning

at that moment of intense
sun

in life's regret

downtown in slush

•

in the park I was thinking and can't say it

the
melancholic twist of truth that I'll never
get to know enough of you to think anything else but
what I do.   therefore . . .

mark cynically, that I can't
work the   s   on Garcias possessive.

 Garcias'   Garcia's

•

January 2000,   no illusions
not called
typing anymore

the world
a contradiction of attempts at connection to it /

I crave loneliness as its opposite

time: as matter /   steam from the tub
my empty thought a slight revelation at the haze
of polluted red

I miss my green Underwood.   it implied its own time
& that future would wipe it out

        •

in the snow, no further out
than when I wandered as
a child

one horizon leads
to the next

snow   –

mobile blazed trail, in seconds
where
they want to go

noise /   *power*

the instant   churned

        •

no punctuation for the heart!

diminished in the global sense
so much caring becomes diminishment /

failure.

you won't finally care.

invest.

be somewhere else

stupid

•

you're probably right
to the things I can't admit

so
whatever I thought or felt
tossed away

simply, we agreed to skate
in whatever we don't
want to say, try

again, junctures not unlike
me in the closet in 1951

amidst the shoes, leather & dark
till I was found

and pulled out

•

pot is burned.   my fault &
that the smell remains

to remind me of *all* I
did

& did not reveal in 40 years to ask

forgiveness

it's really just a complete sense
of isolation & not in much control, so therefore –

I think of driving
into the future:

everything rage

but for the miniscule community –
instants of

us going against the global manufactured to raise
the collective chant:

fuck it

•

together we won't know where to go

•

/ or today
those skates bought circa 71.

stiffness gone, or never there, all energy propelled
bends   my ankles

I'm winded
when I thought: *this ice oval will clear*
my head

give little buds of *one* good thought /

in the millennium

my aging
exaggerated

by the fight against it

•

Sunday: *Forests for the World*   —   ski
the lake

skirt its edge, clear headed to see the
conspire: nature — streaked cloud
to pure

/ light

no mind to see

•

it's over

the table — where light meets
dark, the vice versa

defined as time
every thing about to be
invisible: the countenance of flesh, language

departure

I'll weep later / thank
the blessing of some kind of surety
gone

bless the balance the music brings
(backdoor club Granville Street, the year 2000

life gone under

more allowance of
the necessary:

Gerry Gilbert on
a bike

•

it stinks.

last night's crap

in the air, 30 years later
Husky Oil never once to care

exhaust pipe goes.   70 bucks   I don't
care

no self righteousness   assumptions
of exemptions

to make a difference in the hum &
buzz and electric surge

•

valentines — I'm late /   chocolates
half price

I buy   a box

& flowers   chosen in the instant
I see the buds are closed /   imagine them in water

open on

table of our house.   later think: *the bonus points
almost add to nothing*

— prize objects /
the zero of their own attempted instant

what is good?

particular and mechanical
disintegrations

that made to outlast, a slander: those well
made boots . . .

o

in the exhale
of mundane thought,

complete

time goes in / the space
it begins /

•

e-mail pile

anxiety

too late to return broken razor,
the phone

not working

so goes better my ending

naked /

to the world, smaller, acoustical,

musical

visible.

A Walk

taken again to that margin of a world
ETHEL WILSON, *Swamp Angel*

a walk

— knowing
this risk   to believe   as a walk to some edge
returns its body

eliminates

— the darkness
illusions unfulfilled

so the mind
— loops to knowing

the rose smell & its disappearance —
I wanted against the thought of loss

•

it   does matter

•

the sexual rose — pungent
wild park   of wild roses

returns us changed

(how love but with belief
we are for its purpose

that the prison contain
so each be lung

redemption

as air   that contains the rose

•

breathe benign
thankful you might know in time

& kiss to eternity /

define   darkness

conditions — undescribed
that lead to humour and trust

as ebb & flow lead to   anything
better

that we may get above
the guards

the summons to appear

•

& since we were not meant to be,   *why not hope?*

& know time is a liver, sliver & arrow of wind to
make a neutral soul surmise its own disguise

to come alive, *alive.*

and know we can again
love, even if it be thought it could not be

•

I wanted not to go, necessarily, went
warily, without a
care

drunk

next to a
Scottish rhododendron, whispered, *give me back
my heart*

wondered where it went   without blame or fault.

(in this life
I think the worst,
consequence then comes as diminished surprise

to only pay half, or nothing of
what you thought

owed

weakness the willingness, the offer to pay anything, to be
taken off the hook

•

this has been   as a
walk —
life with you

mythical /

in its endurance

— a petal /   becomes a cosmos

•

a worry wort looks at flowers
to push the residual
bits and pieces to life — a sense of beauty.

who in a notebook fails   to say or record
simple fact:

cruel father, bears gentler child (your
love of plants, the fertile hard fruit you'd
place in the sun like you did the other day, like you did
over 30 years ago, reminds me

of my own need

my shortcomings lead . . .
you see it cannot be said, remains a wish

yet real love proclaims it
in the silence of our bending
to water plants, to touch (I was never
good at, being of such family I'm in strange opposition to
though no less love.

body & soul, now proclaim it
— accurately as
carving to yield a cave
time's cave   with light   near the end

•

I went   left

toward love
and what I believed /

those years of darkness & all I could not say or know
or make known, to realize, be made worse by recognition
of what I needed to resolve

•

are greener pastures over the hill in a storm cloud?   in
Scotland I didn't quite know

a long way to walk

                            — up the glen
did I give you my tam to wear?

I was worrisome in that constant moving dark cloud
that led me to darker places.   met others   lost along the way

extant, we were

all alive enough to want it more so — preposition to pronoun

to clothe legitimacy

decency / generosity

                •

the female voice became my tether, motionless.   weightless
as motive.

though dark little, those evil in the cave.   dark little those evil
in the cave.

so I would know and vow to overcome

my own dark self

in time decay — & endless day out to desert / metaphorical sea.
still to complain *water is not the world*

            •

to guess at
where the walk will end.   near the sea?
by that ancient grave in Anglesey?

no answer when the mind's in motion toward its
awkward testament

— *it will not end*

•

what is any journey partially but a description
        of its length —

did you really see the world

hungover in England?

the sick know what it is to want a home & see
themselves,   the source of their faith that they may some day
return.

they wait with a heart
more forgiving.

the others   come untethered
see the world wanting it.

I'm in between

though as years ago, as yesterday smelled clover
at the intersection & was rushed back — my
Anglia to 37th

early sixties, we fucked in grass.

in sexual love

I compromised to your female harder edges.

a softy,

makes possible
the change

of heart —

•

did we, 35 years later sitting on the wicker on the
   porch,   change our life?   decide

let's be our knowing

that leaky trail to the —

what's the name of those flowers,
& why my worry,   why,   what am I late for?

seconds lost
might become your fate (accidents
to love

shift demise to desire

•

how can I make it?

or define the incomprehensible sea of love
amongst the motion of its wrecks /   in the depths

to the other side?

•

am I here?   last night, beautiful light   / burst clouds
I saw

on the green who
would imagine

our unlikely symbiosis: me with range
you with an eye   to become   a pair

wild

cranberries, tart in season

•

I know now
love by its impossible measure
that its denial, equally forms its presence
but that the imagination still seek its flesh / will not still

the human cry —

how name the sorrow
that defines you
as those who define
their well being in selfish smugness

we know the world will go

•

it was not the distance gone nor what I saw regaled
my change of mind;   it was the edge

a margin to

the changeable energy of uncertainty that yields to this thought:

to be without you

a simultaneous sense of life / its
obliteration

•

I walk   from the hole

to love /

the mirrored edge
that cast me

Sex at 52

it was not so much sex

•

at 52

a change of mind — the body, to let it ache
elsewhere

sex at 52

as the first fuck,   as the last

•

think like an orgasm in selfish exchange

is it we get closest here
or furthest apart

so caught in the ecstasy / two
beings slick & wet   abandoned   to the thing itself /

as want

of physical testament — adornment in the
human condition?

•

in fucking,   aim to disappear / each
to *become   appearance*, a wholeness as part of an
illusory cosmology

•

we are nowhere   in this wanting
come together

to see
the double plunge —   as primordial / promise

•

women see bones and hard flesh angular,
whole being in a step or glass held in talk, angled a certain way,
or a voice   as a promise of care or whatever it is would draw you.

men /   *same*

to hazard a guess: there is no angle in paradise

a curve we don't deserve: *sex at 52*, in life

I had to go into the dark to be alive.

then I was   held   in a graveyard,   lay blind
drunk on a wet lawn, at dawn.

all I ever wanted

learn love   almost ruined by our expectations of it.

at 52

•

this embrace gives the momentary world the edge you think
is paradise, and our ruin becomes its meaning

and welds us silver in a ring of virtue and trust
unerring faith, given at last our sense of a last
divinational pause

at 52 it was a multiple — might as well say an angel's voice

to pull my winged heart to the wells of thought: disappear to
come alive.   to be nothing

reveals

everything you forgot.   & thus at 52, a kind of recognition
immediate trust leading to kindness though

noise —   time rattling at your soul & your revenge, to stay it,
to fuck, to hold & revere the image of this as an absolute when
the absolute has fallen apart.   this is our revenge

sex at 52

•

in   the drunken fuck

flowers / emerge fecund from slate on
the roof across

and memory of want when the eye exploits
the hills / to you   a curve ahead of me in the heather
the sheep, the rhododendrons, the gorse, the thistle.

sex at 52   attempts to deny

my lost ego —   death looming

sex

expansive restoration, this little hope of fools and
cry babe toughs

must learn to forgive
make betrayal the sweet meat . . .

a ragged truth to go on

in beds in fields in grass

•

sex at 52

•

what I do, driven that it gets
no better, a world of thin design

of what men have done and said,   becomes opposite in the
obsessive blind reliance on their gizmos.   in this lie I'm driven

to the fuck,   a joke

so the coat leaks   & lets me
to the weather / dull suburbs as landscape when I look out
the bus — *despondency*
to sex
          as a force against it.

•

sex at 52 —

accept terror as a line dissolved
in the chance for beauty,
to know /

what it is

that wait for space to take its shape — *men / women* — skewered
time that bids farewell: (sex at 52 without you

I can't imagine.

            •

sex at 52

plead   no love —

        to leave

An Unfinished Theology

the angel   an attention become belief

•

a particular place (False Creek — a point, a bay with boats in the
gray, I thought, or think it now, the heart — *this cliché*
contains   its loss,

— yet gives.

authenticity,   momentary point of being

ferries   what appears

•

do you want to
walk?

the angel asks

how do you want to be loved?

(death disappear turn its head.

then I rose to an edge of being

and the shadow in my mind
pushed aside the rest

and I saw
desire,

itself the thing I desired.

to say *love,* to dismiss that against it.

•

it is you
                    transfiguring
the gray that lights us;   jewels in my eyes, parts of bone,
splinter, feather, ginkgo, goose, — a wish for flight though
flesh be gone.   so we will wish it, know it   pain & sweetness of
it, an ideal we dismantle to fill the hole of want & of what be left
of time

measure minutes, the unfair ticks of eternity, the second opening
to glimpse mortal body, beauty   of no words
to say it   & language of all we'll have to hold to

the inaccuracies   to allow

the unfinished theology embodied in this space of thought that
attracts / detracts in a simultaneity we know not what
to call.   all I could say in a whisper —

god bless you.

•

what did the angel ask who has come in mortal form —

are you all right?

I answered torment & pleasure of space & time   (energy of
the impossible that makes us look / see again, to reverse

become.

the angel said: *I came to love*

                     by examination of

         its shadows

     •

so
     in
shadows we'll be found   our point
of loss
to illumine dark   in these shadows
& the light beyond

there is no heaven, but the procreative
moment.

I address you

angel

          — a prayer,

        desire
     self and world unfinished

It Can't be Said

for the memory of Ben McKinnon (1922 – 2000)

it can't

be said

living, I can't imagine you dying.

•

the window looked west
later, a dust, a skiff — light   March snow.   suburbs
with an elevator, the lake, a bank of Indian
land.   you said:

they want a road.

•

want   a road

into these words, thoughts barely
to notice the nurse pleasant, caring and human in the seeming
cold millennial politic versus this kind of care

you dripping into a bag — bladder pain
pressure, TV up to your right —   nonsense to waste what little
time our small talk must contain

what can I say: without cliché.   I
swear beneath my breath — angered by a finality
undescribed,

ourselves, I think later, today, two weeks ahead in life after
you died, not that death is exit from time: *it is*

time, — *not* a vale, but a folding in space without wind / air
when the last instant is a burst as if the beginning of the world
itself *now* reversed and only of itself
as fact in all its puzzlement.

how to go on
to form resolve and be of this body about
to leave

.

I'm taking this razor back

the one I use
to shave you, thinking, I'm this close (though once we hugged
in a parking lot / later a gravesite & you winced   at my move to
intimacy;   therefore, distance & my fear, as they warned, of all
unresolved

.

in a complex, you taught:

root hog or die

.

what can we do but imagine, that our life be described
in whatever instant of thought becomes image (as the
picture of me, the baby, in your arms — you sitting on the
root cellar door with . . .

time ahead.

this time   that I now inhabit   to cancel
my days.

•

no image /   in truth

no subject but time that contains our demise
so that my attempt at the invitation to place a letter in your
grave —

I found, instead, a botched copper horse bulged in a desert scape
that I tooled in an early grade;   you had it

copper to last forever.   I tacked it to my wall

your empty grave

grieving, grieving
the resolve of the unresolved —

& only this outside guess
at your thought:
the conscious measure of each shallow breath, pressures
anxieties, indignities, embarrassments, false
hope. you said:

I'm in my second childhood

•

I'm nowhere /   an unknown somewhere   where

—   my attempts
for location,   a wordless elocution — a lament
in
silence to let image, solid and *only* of the world — enter the eye
to take my heart from this,   left bereft
and fatherless

(that now I must . . .

in the face of it   see a bit of a joke
in our practical concerns.

check my mutual funds

      •

legacy almost
wordless (that day you
on the river in the rain at that point where I thought
this is miserable

you said

it's all right with me.

so I take the rain / my future
without you

      •

you said: *thanks for coming*

I said goodbye twice without looking

the phone to you rang . . .

you died

and I came into this world again,   a strange
and conscious birth

without word, without road

without a father.

Surety Disappears

surety
disappears

begs
to word

silence — its meaning

to the world

•

want

to see in an orb the imagined world

against   / abasement

a voice   to say: *come
up   these stairs to light*

•

there *is*   a voice
a light   /
between ditch and road, as the drunk in Dublin, myself

sensed human good

in Temple Bar

— a stranger
hugged me

& my abandonment reminded
I was in it /

— a life /

to

hold

against /   false arrangements

know opposites /   not as pain but
source

•

there is no plan but the *moment*.   no end but the moment you
leave

          the past
I dig from

no time
to erase

•

grief
that coming up the stairs I am
— *my father*

•

lacuna
      between want of all
denied / delayed

became my soul
to suffer its own belief

to
be held
in
fear
of loss as loss
itself

unearthed as it is unending as it is the heart intoned
      to the singing breeze
neither wronged nor beaten for it beats
intoned
      hopeless to its measure

is its measure

      •

this bridge of time   where
my girdled word spun
mental

the world
in sigh of disclosure of what it is

I wanted to say

      •

where is my rock in earth's
rocky path

myself?

lost in days disappearing
eternity —

        out of this light
to shadows
    birthed
to shadows birthed to dark
to light to   dark
again

     •

I've begun
sick /   shaken to what love would absorb
that a failure contentious and arranged —
is more bound by the fear that
justifies it.
others cursed ahead
lamp lit

     •

woman the lamp — their curving forms
the world attained   to disappear
as those happy
bonded in smug delight   to the smug energy
they describe

who will
we walk with   to celebrate the siren
of marriage / the announcement that this moment   is our stay
against the rest?

     •

my soul in its
zeal to know

she wrapped me
vanquished   she disappeared in her largesse
that I live

to
wish I return complete

that *we* may live before
the arbitrary cease
us.

     •

will I return

to word and flesh   as care and force
seek us / cast us
as a season returning / ending
so no line exist /   separation,   a body
folding   want to want erased
commingling to the
good?

on the cobbled path   earth
is a
universe
guilds   the nothingness
sheaths   moonlight on
your breast

     •

this beauty

is desire that asks
we bear again
the moment it appears

toss question, what is left:

words, the hole   despondency

to flat epiphany: the face, the form, the voice
turning / mind to buds —
green & spring's sad
goodbye.

        •

my meaning   removed
— every surmise
a disguise

a fool

        •

months later
        on
the trail   I was
sick of my shadowed loneliness, then thought:
        it is my only light

the reality   at gulf of being:

        hope is despair

        •

speechless — a smeared dream:

*joy, the moment of all I wanted, the whole of knowing what I
could not attain of you now appeared.   it was the sense of what
I always knew spoken at last.   we flew this way   together from
the world.*

•

space of sun
light in hall   to xerox room.   love orbs
its instant of escape: *pure being, your life was in itself the all of
expectation without regret in the complex of all of its
aspects,   —   was lived,
    faced*

(our plane   flying low / destined.

a desert below

*(how beautiful you were,   what I knew — smile, body of whole
self contained so nothing now could change the sense of it
presented*

•

a whim of wind & a sense of self I am.   irrevocable;   my
hallucination & illusion — smiling to announce:
        this is a place I'll be

no beginning remembered, no middle not knowing the distance
to its end.
but a kind of traveling — to see
grass and snow

my measure   of meaning

a   gulf — to endeavor shaped
in the simple decry of   complex attainments exact as the risk
to attain them: life at the bearing

edge   I sensed myself
when the accordion
became my desire's pleated air

into the suburb thinking — what becomes in love not
expressed (these minutes we could keep   — redemption

to a hinge of words,   a river of loss come to

the meaning
of itself

·

how else speak but lose

our loss to containment /   refills this window's
crack of light —   our fate to *a containment recognized* —

·

Cottonwood Island — 30 below (March
river hued blue in / north sun
over mill

all energy is the incomplete

this end   in space

(I glance the cutbanks

in the

irreversible luck of time   to make
my heart a memory

Head Out

(A Letter, Essay, Poem — to Cecil Giscombe)

Preface

My friend the American poet Cecil Giscombe and I took part in *Philly Talks* #18: A Dialogue with Contemporary Poets, in the Rosza Centre at the University of Calgary on February 2, 2001. The reading, talk and discussion took place with a live audience (and an audio webcast for those who wanted to listen and ask questions live via the *Philly Talks* web connection, phillytalks. org).

Short weeks before the live event Cecil and I exchanged new writing that became the focus for the *Philly Talks* newsletter web document. This material was accompanied, also, by responses / reviews / reactions to our work by three other poets: Wayde Compton, George Elliot Clarke, and Giovanni Singleton.

What follows here is my written response to Cecil Giscombe's e-mails to me prior to the reading: it is a response to Cecil's poems / poetics / & concerns as I see them. In this version the text has been edited and Joy McKinnon's Giscome photos added. I do, however, prompt any interested reader to see the full context of *Philly Talks* #18 — which as a whole consists of the poems, essays, statements, e-mails, queries, and written responses that arose out of the live web cast discussion.

I'm not sure that during the talk / discussion part of the event Cecil & I made any teleological advances — even without the pressure to do so; however, we both agreed the next day of feeling — the word we simultaneously blurted out in laughter — was: *stupid*. When in the range of intelligent, huge, hairy, and difficult questions that we were asked — concerns of place, race, meaning, form, content and the intents of poetry — our answers, or a least mine as I remember them, went out by the seat of my pants. If only had we *more* time to *think*! To say what we *really* mean! To revise the spontaneous inaccuracies *with* felicity! etc. ...

Nevertheless:

never apologize, I once heard it said:
risk to let the voice and writing stand.

Head Out

Cecil: On the phone I asked: *What are we going to do?* — a
question regarding the why, when, what and where of the *Philly
Talks* event. We both began to laugh / nervously. But this to say,
you've plunged ahead and given me a wonderful essay / letter,
new poems and notes I'll respond to here — make a plunge
that I hope gets me to somewhere and you — to connect our
journeying / returns

into the large concerns of our talks: *poetry &* . . .

the complex practice of it that we may stand *reaffirmed /
ashamed* together, also in a kind of happiness and laughter —
bound as we are to attempt its secret / lead our lives by it —
baffled dumb / to want / any need to journey / return.

Ten years ago: you in Normal, Illinois, and me in Prince George,
B.C. — an unlikely geographical connection, your voice on
the phone — smooth, subdued, quiet, intelligent and polite
— introducing yourself via George Bowering's suggestion
that you contact me — you a poet with a project, making a
simple request: you needed an invitation and a letter to support
your plan to track the black explorer and miner John Robert
Giscome's journey and life in the mid 1800's *viz.* his presence in
B.C., based on your serious premise of a family blood tie.

J.R. Giscome / C.S. Giscombe

And within a year, there you were in the parking lot of the
Downtowner Motel in Prince George. Did I wave first or
did we wave simultaneously? We gave no physical clues for
identification. I knew from scant historical information that J.R.
Giscome was black / you couldn't be white (I'd have been very
suspicious if you were!)

the   blood   ties.

now, here, your return via John Giscome to begin the long
journey — almost a decade ahead of you — into the poem:

Giscome Road

our immediate connection / spontaneous

difficult talk / easy talk. We, familiar with similar materials or
lack of them, and *questions* — and a sense of a share in a cursed
journey, if it were not for the almost promise that its very activity
is what could equally save anyone on it.

We talked

into the night — back porch beer epiphanies / and over the
years of our talks to a kind of necessary knowledge — as if by
articulating a shared skill, concern, and practice, each step ahead
be taken more assuredly — give simultaneous courage in the
foolish prompt to risk

words

the wilderness   the nothing

dumbly /   head out

as early miners packing each thing for a journey into vast
unknowns, up the physical canyons, through miles of bush I can
barely walk a block through. (Cecil, that day on the Giscome
Trail in the sheer and wonderful context of the "historical"
moment, being with you, I was also being bled by many species
of carnivorous bugs — and in fear noted trees shredded by recent

hungry bears. How far did we go until we got the idea: this,
now, *here*, the literal Giscombe Trail / *his* portage on
to Summit Lake / the water
shed divide at 54'40" — longitudes and latitudes of history.
I watched
you swim out   quite a way.

our subject?   What tools, what corporeal / mind / necessity
let us start with an agreement, spit out without a thought, yet
a thought we continuously return to by virtue of its curiosity
— to a "theme" of sorts: "this is a place we decided, *but there's
nothing here.*"

   right   and   wrong

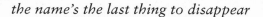

   the name's the last thing to disappear

Giscome/Giscombe

no more Saturday nights there

Who cares in the expectation of dislocation as normal in the
Canadian northern corporate practice and ethos? In recent
history (the 50's) the Cheslata indians "removed" from their land
by the Alcan / Kemano project, given scant hours notice before

the flood. Giscome emptied on scant notice in 70, (there's a long list of other towns and people) — and most recently Tumbler Ridge* where I write this (a coal mining town shutting down) — a place in a huge transition that very much attracts me. In its disintegration to become a ghost town for ecotourists, old-age pensioners, snowmobilers, poets, and misfits — I begin to feel, illusionary or not, a sense of being, temporarily, out of dislocation: these beautiful mountains, and air and cheap real estate — a real place in the detritus after they've gone, whoever they are (innocent or not). I'm thinking of the *what&who* in the ruthless discard of primal economy. What of value can be kept?   What's changed in America, the north —

here

& Giscome, the town in 71, where Joy and I felt *not* at home, but that this place *was* a home; she photographed each house, street, church, train station, mill, machines / machinery and *every thing* abandoned.

---

* Tumbler Ridge was becoming a ghost town in 2000. The world price of coal dropped and allegedly the TR supply was dwindling, so the mining companies shut down / moved out. By 2005, world prices went high enough to attract several companies who have since opened or re-opened mines. TR is now integral to the new global economy — namely China's requirement for resources in its move to the next stage of industrialization. The oil and gas reserves in the northeast BC region and the additional economic activity this generates means the local economy is, as they say, thriving (but not without, also, new threats of serious social and ecological costs).

On one of those trips to Giscome I drove out along Eaglet Lake
until I feared going on. This sense of nothing ahead. A road to
end without reason. Where would I be in this momentary terror
— my soul I literally sensed, *gone* — cast from the earth into
the diffuse centerless light. Is this *the* dislocation, or *the* terrified
connection — (poem, now, as portage of our own necessity and
making — words as map, tendril, trail and path to return to
where? — the poet going forward / back on a syntactical bridge
only strong enough, *in* this necessity — because we're traveling
light — to carry only his / her own weight? The words / words
got you *to Giscome Road.*

no backdrop

here

you made words / large fact of a world once blank, *almost* empty,
almost nothing / went back —
    ward for / word into terrestrial multiples: Jamaica to the
babbling old man / — a long lost Giscom(b)e on a front porch —
knew nothing you needed *to know*: no evidence at the primary
source: *therefore*

•

Cecil Giscombe on a ten-speed bike, poet peddling into the centerless light: Jamaica, North America, Normal, Prince George, Giscome, the prairie Midwest — into

diffuse light.

    (feet, head, and eye

into —

      nowhere / somewhere, far, two directions, with open return. into & out of . . .

      describing it

        head out

Endnote

Many of the thoughts in my improvisation bounce from Cecil's title *Into and Out of Dislocation*. I think I'm just beginning to understand it (beyond the medical description of Cecil's injured / dislocated arm as described in his book) — in terms of his life and writing as an African American writer in America, *and* Canada. The title poses a great millennial question: if we know, with varying degrees of intensity the arbitrariness of what being *into dislocation* is, (aren't we *all* in it, or about to be?) — then what is it to be *out of dislocation*? The *place* this question imagines is open to what human values we would presently wish to define it as (a real *place* without compromise or illusion?). What presence & location do humans anywhere have in the current psycho / sociology of what has happened / happening here / anywhere you care to look? The world's largest clearcut in the Bowron valley is 40 minutes from Prince George — large, invisible; it's "nothing", they say. The unrecorded world, *this* close, (20 minutes from Giscome) — yet, minimal fact given the human dislocations & disturbance of the larger daily world eco / human diaspora. A question:

the task of poetry?

poetry /

What I've wanted. The poem itself (an artifact / *real* place) — & I've also wanted the very moments of its act & its energy (integration / location) — to include, as well, a necessary, disintegration of its conscious *and* unconscious premises? By this I mean the practice I think I see in George Stanley's new work: he writes / builds a line that seems dismantled *at the same time* — to reveal accurate processes of mind and life moving to their jagged truths. This want of a new world! This want of the new poem! *Get a life!* I hear them say while "real life goes on" into and out of the language and world at hand — *into & out of . . .*

I think the task — & Cecil so large among the others I admire for taking it on — is to break form, break ground, *be* ground (*not* backdrop), so that when the radio is on, the static clears.

Now voice and music are heard, and the pleasure of the information to make what need be known and said, visible.

Notes / Works Cited for *Head Out* & Endnote

The line "journeying and returns" is the title of an early book by bp Nichol.

The line "reaffirmed / ashamed' is from William Carlos Williams' poem proclaiming: "I am a poet! I am a poet!"

References to "this is a place, we decided . . ." is from Cecil's essay "Border Towns, Border Talk", published in Beeler & Horne, eds., *Diverse Landscapes: Rereading Place Across Cultures in Contemporary Canadian Writing* (Prince George: UNBC Press, 1996).

"The name's the last . . ." is from *Giscome Road* (Normal IL: Dalkey Archive Press, 1998).

Various titles I've taken from Cecil Giscombe's *Prairie Style* (Chicago, IL: Flood Editions, 2008).

"Real life goes on" is a Robert Creeley quote on the back jacket of Cecil Giscome's *Into and Out of Dislocation*.

Post Response: Supplement to *Philly Talks* #18

My job as a poet is to see and to unravel arbitrary and pre-conceived notions and definitions of reality, including what I might conjure as my own: the poet can't help but do this because of the very nature of the energy & process of the language that's chosen him or her. What has been mapped by manipulative and self-interested forces, from whatever source or reason, is firstly what the poet must at the most rudimental start of the thinking and writing process attempt to take apart. I must find myself asking unanswerable questions; there is no choice. The poem is a process that defies the static, the set, the static arbitraries that herd most populations through life and language. The poem is verb: there are no nouns in nature: nature has neither centre nor periphery.

Place becomes for me the perception of that moment when my eye sees an instant and then sees through it / knows it; the poem moves at it, in it, becomes both it and not it. This written instant is of a / the world unmapped, immediate and excitingly incomprehensible, (now there and visible for "gradual awareness") and by that fact more real in its assertion than the lower-order uses of language that manipulate to create static, noise & stasis. In these manipulated claims of the "real world" by those obsessed with power, the dramatic premise is that once a thing ceases to move it is easier to kill (literally or metaphorically) — the poet included. If Cecil and I share anything, I hope it is a clear sense of these margins, bounds and conditions and that we are neither black nor white (but a multiple of complex human activity which may include these designations*) — while in the heart and moment of the process of seeing and writing, terrified or not, in this necessary disappearance of the preconceived.

This is part of a poem I wrote in the 1970's that Cecil referred to — having an importance to him — shortly after we met.

... it should be easier, so I go
back
          — some uttered language, rooted in the void,

as driving N.E. of Giscome — to McGregor — not making it
   — running low
on gas — the sun blinding — a sense of being

                    nowhere,   suspended & scary.   the truck
moves along,
                    between mountains, a train, slag heaps, (a copper
                    mine? thus
                              the green ring that edges the lake?

such descriptions, without a meaning — or I am without
     a meaning,

                         not clearly, at 35
                                   driving ...
                                             (*The the.* 88)

* I'd like to question large and assumed categories and nominalisms even further as when poet George Stanley writes to announce: "I am not a man ..."(68). Similarly, here is Leonard Cohen saying: "... in an embrace you're neither man nor woman — you forget who you are. Once you have experienced yourself as neither man nor woman, when you are reborn into the predetermined form which you inhabit, you come back with the residue of experience or the residue of wisdom which enables you to recognize in the other extremely familiar traits". (Crouch 21).

Here is part of Cecil Giscombe's poem "Far":

> It's that this far inland the appearance of a fox is more than metaphor. Or the appearance is a demonstration. Sudden appearance, big like an impulse; or the watcher gains a gradual awareness — in the field, taking shape and, finally familiar. The line of sight's fairly clear leaving imagination little to supply. It's a fact to remember, though, seeing the fox and where or, at night, hearing foxes (and where). The fox appearing, coming into view, as if to meet the speaker.
>
> Push comes to shove. Mistah Fox arriving avec luggage, sans luggage.
>
> *(Inland, 5)*

I see these lines as a conjunction in our thinking and writing — poets moving into / out of sudden appearance to trace the fact of a dislocated moving place.

Works Cited for Post Response

Crouch, Leanna. Ed. *One on One: The Imprint Interviews* (quote from "In the Field", Leonard Cohen interviewed by Barbara Gowdy), Toronto: Somerville House, 1994.

Giscombe, C.S. *Inland*. Oakland CA: Leroy 7 Chapbook Series Two, 2001.

McKinnon, Barry. *The the*. Toronto: Coach House Press, 1980.

Stanley, George. *At Andy's*. Vancouver: New Star Books, 2000.

For a chronological history of the town of Giscome see J. Kent Sedgwick's *Giscome Chronicle: The rise and demise of a sawmill community in central British Columbia 1912 – 1976*. Prince George: College of New Caledonia History Series, 2008.

A Note on the Photographs

Joy McKinnon took the Giscombe photographs that appear here.
In the early 70's when we heard the town was being abandoned
& bulldozed — as is a common history with Canadian company
towns — Joy decided to make a photo record before the town's
impending fate. Taki Bluesinger, a Vancouver photographer and
media artist, was visiting at the time; he also took an interest
in our project to create a visual document of a place about to
disappear. In conjunction with Joy's black and white photo
document, Taki and I convinced a colleague at the College of
New Caledonia with a pilot's licence to take us up for an aerial
view. It was a bumpy ride with Taki at the controls of an old-
style video camera the size of a small suitcase, panning the town
below. I've heard that someone in Taki's family has his archive. I
hope the shaky video film still exists as part of it — in the black
and white of what we saw those many years ago.

APPENDIX I
Bayday

This poem was written shortly after the town of Giscome was evacuated and bulldozed. A local radio station in Prince George, most likely CKPG at the time, was running advertisements for the Hudson's Bay Company's "Bayday" promotion which involved a roving car equipped with a loudspeaker that randomly stopped at various houses at various times of the day. If a "lucky" resident happened to hear and respond to the bullhorn line: *you've got 55 seconds* etc. . . . they'd win some kind of prize. My sense was that if someone in Giscome came into the street for the "prize" they might have had their house bulldozed while their backs were turned. The italicized radio lines were jotted and spliced in as I wrote.

       Giscome   shack town, no more
Saturday nights there.   one man remains

          to watch the mill.   he knows nothing
     can be carried easily
             away.   but the people willingly
   were
          on one month's notice . . . *the answer to their*
         problem . . . CBC

      (some houses are livable yet
        bulldozers to scrape it all away, as if some natural
        cycle is at work

              but people   people lived
there
        as CBC goes on:
                    we are capable of understanding
                    the culture . . .
                                etc.

        as the local radio goes on jingling
and jangling
                the nerves:

                    you've got 55 seconds
                    to come out & see what

                    you've

                    won.

The Upper Fraser Road

from *Giscome Road*. C.S. Giscombe

(the Upper Fraser Road makes a long S across the tracks & goes on.)

first view:

the church with its giant cross, the steeple rising above trees & visible too, through those, a red Blazer wch I assumed — from a quarter mile off — was many parked cars or indicative of them, it being Sunday morning

following:

the 5 houses,

Giscome School w/ its windows all decorated for Halloween & the banner inside WELCOME TO GISCOME & their gym shoes in cubbyholes visible too through one window,

the CN trackside bldgs,

the single vehicle, the Blazer, parked out from the church right past where a little dirt road stopped,

the floating green edges of the lake past the flat where apparently the mill was

(the district inhabited if sparsely, unhaunted).
(the view on out Eaglet Lake at the mountains

Notes Incorporating 2 Lines By Barry Mckinnon

from *Giscome Road*. C.S. Giscombe

1

(On the long road back from there I drifted
— I was on my English bicycle—
down through some commotion I made
in the landscape.)

2

there's no center where
similarity would begin

nor annotated wasteland out there leaning

on the easily borrowed heart for an announcement,

there is no-

where to go out there —

3

came to necessarily centerless space, though (or the intimation of
that & out of that the specific, there

4

to which I came up some ways

(I'd come up through a long silence on the way up

to Giscome up the Yellowhead

X miles out of Prince George, NE of there

5

& turned back into the direction I'd come out of,

out of the gap of the landscape there, a
named edge: the juncture of this one little edge
in the line of trees,

the gap of that lake's many edges —

6

no more / saturday nights there

the town bull
dozed but the evidentness on passing even quickly through of
some-

thing having happened there, some things having taken place
there, even people

fucking, say, in the houses (those gone & the few ones left)

or in the fields just past there, . . .

Joy (An Epithalamium)

in my head

a place

where desire contains
the description of its loss —

now, thrown to the moment of dread.

that I did not get *there*, to *that* missed, I, forsaken in

time and hope to revise: make old
to new

a life, and world
with you

that I must speak
what I sense I cannot say
be said: image / you, *the figure*, literal *in* my life
to make *it* my life so I was final — *myself.*

•

I first saw

you —   teenage blur.   *you* in that chance,
hand to breast, the kiss / a relinquishment deep — sexual.
blur of moon —
Volkswagen — river bank
primordial, visage of
self in moment of consummation / world
entered, defeated to the self become.

love was its articulation to the complex of itself.   our
dream: only to say *it is*

the breast, the curve of hip I saw then I saw
& pled   help us   in this recognition: hell of

forms   separation.

so mindless was I   followed / loved   abandoned
to believe I could be, to speak, to be
with you.

.

memory a
loss now kindled
to talk   these years to see ourselves

in love's attempt — defined.   detailed

you
in 64 — as now, love   then also its threat (leaving it
that I become
measured   when I think: *the others*

I break to jealous heat: *the thought*

the loss of you

— like a substance   the river is drowned   is itself
is time *is* loss

.

this dialogue drifts.   *come up*
come up the stairs with me — please hear
this testament against our grief:

loss, against loss,   to make a
life with you by shards / remains

a plea

a move to love /   one's time & language
to reach again

the body — sensed / riven
by days we balanced the beam
of love / in domestic routine —

but wild we were to risk what we could lose: *each
other*, that the distance made each return a measure that now
to sense

*fathoms, a surface, a light, a life
somewhere.*

•

yesterday, wanted to *say*,   be *believed* to cessate
its need, to see,   all unreal mistaken for the real.

your body, every moment
of it, as entrance, where

I vanish   be found — *vanished*

do you see me?   that what you see is what I believe

I see myself, *am I the belief of what you see?*

•

I had a life

I had no bus   to take

I was outside   to ask how faith now bloom to possibility
of faith

so I measured the changing light —

waited

in space

•

you did not want me

or my beauty, or mistook the world's attraction as what unfolds
to be

as a place it takes to leave (a porch, a car, a bed, walking to
Vancouver blind
— waking to that recognition I believed   unable to
bear: *I wanted you*

concomitant: myself in its loathing echoed a soul without itself

•

born in fear — I invent a place
with exit near.   when in sleep
in a dream I will believe — wakes love to

marry us
again

Bastard File

Radio On

radio on, thinking
> *I'll write a story about gardening*, for Stan
Chung — or George Bowering

> or —

or thinking: where's that noise from? *or*
my old friend David Phillips out in the mud of mid life
resentful though he has the biggest heart I know, clear
mind honed in anger. it's maybe time. let's loosen up, go back to
love (ashamed at the world.

— "he loves the learning and the teaching for their own sake"
> — (CBC)

me: it's Feb. 16, — and a hangover enough to let the half sick
mind write out its course. or, it's too cold at 30 below, to go out,
though the sun is high, bright — and beautiful, but you must
constantly think, stink of polluted air. perhaps, there is no hope.
(yet live daily &
> sing the body

> *electric*

•

"the squids eye" is similar to what? no different than the
statement: *I can't understand what he does*   or to think the
future of poetry is past. (as in that garden I was so dumb, I didn't
know how to rake. *make many little piles* & while in the rain
wear *proper* gear — and sense the foliate world.

I turned the radio off and hit "save." "untitled" becomes, "poem"
& I wonder in this task how best get out of the way of what
breaks in. I go back in revision, turn on the heat cube
& drink from a Tim Horton cup.

•

furnace on. 38 below / a letter being read, "there were tears in
my eyes."

life's ease. distractions. but in the kitchen coming out into the
intensity of the dining room sun, I thought, this is the kind of
day you may die — slight momentary sense of wellbeing
in the body's earned space. I won't worry. by now it's ten
o'clock and I think I know

I'd rake one big pile. old Tom smoked, bowled / waited for
retirement: *make little piles. don't work so hard.*

today: or all day, my old black radio propped in the wood — I
chop, clear snow in the 20 below. sense of / *I won't do
school work.* how many years have I wanted only to live
my life,   or / on the ski trail with Noel, I yell ahead: *I think I've
just started to sense pleasures, enjoyments — embodiment of the
fundamental human and open heart.* actually, it was something
I said about "12 years gone" — tyranny of self in systems of this
world. but here: the woods, the isolate, animals tracks and
cracked trees (all whites, shades of it, and darks

— arc of northern sky —

3 Lines: Gender Studies (a collaboration)

I am not a man

my mother calls me
daughter

I am my father

George Stanley
Ken Belford
Barry McKinnon

Transliteration: *Bushed* to *Lost Along the Way*

Sometime in the early 90's I got a letter from a professor at Sichuan University describing his literary project: to select Canadian poems for a Chinese anthology. He found my poem "Bushed" in Margaret Atwood's anthology *The New Oxford Book of Canadian Verse in English* and wanted permission to reprint it for his proposed *Selected Canadian Lyrics*. I sent off a quick note to say yes and forgot about it.

In 1995 I got a copy of the book and curiously searched through its 190 pages to see what my poem looked like graphed in Chinese. I couldn't read a word, but the overall company of poets felt good: George Bowering, Daphne Marlatt, John Newlove, Margaret Avison, Al Purdy — 33 Canadian writers, each with a short poem translated for millions of Chinese readers.

Later, chatting with the writer Calvin Wharton in Vancouver, I mentioned the anthology and that I was curious to hear what "Bushed" was saying in Chinese. Calvin offered to ask his partner Lian Zhang to do a translation from the Chinese ideograms (*without, we agreed, letting her see my original poem in English*). Lian agreed to this and translated the Chinese version of "Bushed" into "Lost Along the Way" (and also included a translation of the Chinese translator's notes about my "unknown biography" and "his idea".

I'm moved and cheered by Lian's transliteration from "Bushed's" dark mood to something more sanguine. Such delight at the surprise of the borderless light poetry looks for / the beauty it finds.

Bushed

I am in a desert
of snow. each way
to go, presents an equal
choice, since the directions, &
what the eye sees is the same

if there were some sticks, you would
stay & build a house, or
a tree would give a place to climb
for perspective. if you had a match, when
the wind didn't blow, you
would burn the tree for warmth, if
the wind didn't blow & you had a match

there is this situation where love
would mean nothing. the sky is
possibly beautiful, yet the speculation
is impossible, & if you could sing, the song
is all that would go

anywhere

麦金农

迷　途

我正在大雪覆盖的荒漠上
每条小径都是平等选择通向远方
因为每个方向和放眼所见都是一样

如果这里有一些木棒
你就留下来，建造一间住房
如果这里有一棵树生长
你就爬上树去朝远方眺望
如果你有火柴，风也不扬
你就燃烧这棵树来暖暖身上

真有这样的情况
爱情不将任何意义附上
天空多么美丽空旷
在这里不可能沉思默想
如果你能够放声歌唱
那歌声定将传遍四面八方

　　巴里·麦金农（Barry Mckinnon，1944—　　）
生平事迹待考。这是一首具有现代派特色的抒情诗，
所描写情景的时间地点不明确，诗人的感情也没有
在诗中得到直接的表露，他只是用象征、暗示的手
法去引起读者的联想和感受，委婉曲折地传达了自
己的思想：即使是处于困境中，也不要灰心丧气，要
努力创造条件、发扬乐观精神，去战胜逆境带来的
艰难和挫折，开拓美好的未来。

Lost Along the Way

I am in a deserted wilderness covered with snow
every road is an equal choice towards the distance
because whatever you can see, as far as your eyes can see
in every direction, is the same

If there are some sticks
you will stay and build a house
if there is a tree growing
you will climb to the top and look into the distance
if you have matches and there's no wind
you will burn this tree to warm your body

So this can be true: love has no attached meaning
the sky is so beautiful and spacious
and here it's impossible to be silent and thoughtful
if you can let your voice go to sing as loud as you can
then your song will be carried to every corner of the world.

Translator's note

His biography is unknown.

This is a lyric poem in a modern style. It's not clear where and
when the poem is written and the poet's own feeling is not
directly expressed in the poem. He uses only symbolism and
suggestion to help the reader make associations and feel the
experience.

He indirectly expresses his own idea: *Even if you are in a very
difficult situation or are trapped you shouldn't be discouraged
and lose heart. You should try to create positive situations and
be optimistic to defeat all the difficulties and twists brought by
adversity, and open up a beautiful future.*

Lian Zhang's note: The sound equivalents for "McKinnon" in
Chinese, mean, in this order:

Wheat / Gold / Peasant

Writing on the Ridge

for Donna Kane

on the ridge   Donna Kane:
  I thought   you were a paranoid,
but now just cursed

then describes   a red light behind me in the bush
honed in to track me down
that only I can see

she almost agrees, it's *really there*
to find me even here

like undercover cops in New York who busted Jesse and me
in Washington Square for a 3.5% beer, or

border guards as hegemonic device, who ask my name
and deny they did

the paranoid it's true, is the one in true
possession of the facts.

truth & what else goes out
— a life punished without full enrollment
& what gift given   only to bring me trouble

the light: red: hegemonic / demonic
out there   on the ridge, serial and un-
written, tapped to a source

god or devil now somehow   both
the same

o cursed, I'm made to reverse that I'm made to laugh
in my happiness & light

the light and good / not dark nor shade nor
demon red

•

on a dark street in Tumbler Ridge
a dark car   pulls out and follows
every turn

who is that she asks?   *it's the light, the secret*
police.   it's the curse   of what we know

a moment   in the meaning
of life

noise & silence /   these our   words without words

it's the writing on the ridge

she begins to weave the car   in laughter,   this
curse   to be with me.

— flash of red   light behind us

Retinal Detachment

worry to fear.   the line between meaning . . .

only eyes —

      that half a world is dim, milky, sad

I'll do my best — the rest seems a rustling fate in the wall
the arrogance of immunity

impugned /   be humble human at last or
recognize it can be its beginning — the accumulated past -

it's only you.

threat of loss
to become a strength? —

in the hospital silence, waiting — crazed scream /   of wordless
condition

how lucky you are to get
this far   —   *the measure & corporeal recognition: in the land
of the blind the one eyed man is king*

in the trans luscence palpable separation that the world is 3
inches off in my walk and reach — though never, in my
unrequited fate, sensed my
part

such it is with luck
what my mother said looking for the hidden blessing

the hidden blessing

here the silence of the sick to say ... to know their power
not to complain

otherwise, it was May, me on my way, happy to be each day

shadows / detachment — subdued in the palpable enormity
to become all of me

— its diminishment
(if this is about anything

this / distorted
sense of being the blind will see

Prince George (Part One)

for George Stanley

a man in himself is a city — (W.C.W.)

beleaguered / belied   the entrance (*himself,*

   he enters

canyons
  in Hade's hot air

   •

memory of *that* travel
fear   to a sense of life ahead: *the literal city*

busted out — clearing forests / water / air

not form but   what

shapes

     the city   a body
to its
    soul —

   •

down
town tribes —

in their source of
detachment, begin to be
themselves again —   hunt /

history, the millennial weight: no clear stream / or abode
exists:
>   *these   bulldozed souls*

no pity or remorse   to equal what's imagined

handouts on 3rd / the giveaway suits
that clothe them.

oh forest, oh bear — vestigial illumination / the
grins
>   in simple light

they see

>   •

what do *we* see   so clearly in its lack

to see   without image / articulation   — a reason

malls fill / downtown empties / history (capital / frontier
without   human hope: *this is the end, we sing* (crows peck
puke, buckles in the side walk / holes of asphalt, piles of blood

>   •

the man, the city — what parts in
the metaphor, this *way* of dreaming — is the heart a down
town? 1969: the routes (bakery, bread, meat
balls, a pickle and up 4th to
the Astoria (beer — to the Bay, the Northern, Wally West, I.B.
Guest & down to the corner — 2nd & George, the Canada, the
blues, beer,
>   the sense of *here / not here* — this want of places to
be, enter & make
>   sagacious.

•

libraries are for loafers

no blame to local realities. nothing in the way of what doesn't
exist, in the simple mercantile presumptions

the smell of money — the brushcut hero who could make it

the local ethos: *up*
before the rest went to bed / with his bulldozer.

and in a dream of this world woke to

every one / every thing: *fuck   or be fucked*

•

man a city: the female forest —

to imagine the hard / the soft (winter, cycles to summer spring &
fall / bleeding to the genderless human want of tenderness.

root hog or die

when a city becomes its coldest hearts
we live in the illusion of its habitat:

the invisible / visible: the city *you see / did good in*

becomes an old cliché in the toxic mill cloud that fills the bowl
and drifts with the winds — a swirl of stink in the
citizenry / penetrates the corpus while the corporate, that most
visible as the source, least accounted for in the non-existent
public square

I can't breathe

a man must speak, to the threat dismissed, diminished,
coerced by need and want
to sing: *they think they*
do me   no harm.

•

the they.   the *who,* the *us* in the disintegrated
        disintegration — nothing can be known; its own hopeless
statement — *the north / everywhere (but not revealed —*

in this   what?   will we only know the hot day in mid
July 69 into the stink, the heat, the Fraser
bridge / 57 Plymouth packed,

I want to go back

to what humans imagine a version: here / the beer
& coming out of the Barn into that heavy light decide
that moment, to stay.

the apt / penthouse — top floor Trojan Manor $300.00

where do you think you're going? don't want   youse types here.

moved to 1902 Queensway across from Marty's Cafe (shack
— 100 a month (now   Assman's funeral

home —

the city: a world

you entered — sensed body / parts
missing in the civic need the forces disallow — & that called
specious

what saves us — a clarity / conditions born of fog /
suspicion

the love   and hate of uneasy
marriage (man / woman — a city unto themselves

•

what is the source of this thinking? ambiguity, contradiction
power, *that* hidden, conspiracies, pushed
buttons and cliché, until our bodies demotion to banishment.

a shit hole.

•

when are you going to write something good?

•

its activity is also its own resistance: what
to say: what subject, or image — what body part contain
the life / what weakness is strength when

the whole body vomits in nadir (the weakest
now culled once defined: a man vomits

in shame that now the city can not be made

this rotten   dark   soul, a man
a metaphor, a language convinced of its own rhetoric easily
believed (men (the city
its self / fooled
by little stakes / little power (that those governed
men will thrust their outlines — will sacrifice the rest.   will
save themselves
others (those sickest

grin

at any scheme sabotaged by its own impossibility — know the
inventors require such
false faith and fear

•

the city exists / knows itself / cannot change

easily

oh corpus of belched noxious gas
oh corpus of the fruitless / oh corpus of malignment oh
generous corpus of the material world oh
industrial corpus behind the corpus oh corpus of the beautiful
& gentle wind oh corpus in our misaligned prayer oh corpus
of promise and care

oh grid of light, muscled male

•

stomp the tourist's head into the walk — that part psycho
path — the city staggers in a hoedown dance / wild
in iconic illusion of how it sees itself — dressed
to kill any thing in sight

•

arms of the suburbs to father illusion: conglomerate homo unity
turns place / to no place / same place
to exist only in our attempt to define it

•

(off Queensway embarrassment, then disgust — teen hookers to
cross through

the riven world displayed by its line between: *us*
and them

little girls, the man, a city — / homeless

   •

why did you stay?

the density of context peeled was revealed to a momentary
sense of simplicity, that it could be known, and therefore, the
man *could* know himself, being a city: *unto himself,* — its maps
and routes, the air it breathed, capacious unbalance to imply the
need for its opposite: nothing to go on — knowledge without
proof / its energy.

to work
a language in its attempt to equal
the anxious swirl in an angular world of charts, graphs — the
gizmoed patter claimed & believed as real — that any power
required subservience to its whacko notions, be revealed as
public sense: *not agreement, but truth of one's condition faced:*
bloody head in its second of consciousness under the killer's boot
— in metaphoric
drama

be allowed to live.

   •

in the city: Nechako, Fraser
   Husky, Canfor, PG Pulp, Northwood, Intercon, Lakeland,
   CN

city core

body is thought

through parking lot,   plumes
/ trees,
 / polis / man

Bolivia / Peru

This poem is for Viv Lougheed, John Harris, & Joy
— travelers / companions & for those we met along
the way, & for the Bolivian lady who said to us one day:
Que le vaya muy bien — *may it go well with you.*
As it was, we went and went well.

Bolivia

— my life a chunk — language and mud about
to slide as thinking that leads to this:

Bolivia is not a place

in my head, airsick in La Paz, said, *it's a measure*: what the first
and second world take for granted without the 3rd — as an
amazement
when it's finally seen. firstly decide it *does exist* and make an
entrance without preconception; now   no exceptions. who you
are or not is now   arbitrary. scary.

in Lima   you land to trust it enough to leave your pack, go
to the can (young lispy guys hanging out

later, you get mugged

       •

on the plane to La Paz / think *Bolivia Bolivia Bolivia* — how to
conjure sense of this violation to be so far from the familiar
— that down below, land   depressed — stretched, browny   all
the way.

blue rim of lake — Titicaca? — the flashing roofs of tin.
mountain & plains, the people there I imagine.

gringos / — anyone white who looks like us,
— not arrogant but sense of immunity (quickly disappears
at border / guards ask you to fill out visa forms again.

       •

descent. the Alto Plano through slums of dirt, mud and dust, a swirl
of your first — not glimpse of landscape — but flashes / faces, a
kind of teeming human activity, bodies hanging to it — temerity,
— this ... life without hope?

•

thinking goes away. is now   something else

•

not a measure you measure:
(in Bolivia   without a clue, or language — a passport you believe

what literally gets you in and out quickly dissolves (*no*
passport, *no* embassy

you're no one. this is a shithole

•

Plaza de san Francisco. off the micro bus into the swarm of
masked shoe / shine boys / hard breath up market streets   to the
Hostal Arcabucero

cool-out with cheap beer & coca leaves.   take a shit, still good
throw up / put toilet paper in basket w / sign, "Thank you for
your comprehension" — mouth dry, anxious.
altitude / home —
sickness — want   of the familiar — the ...

•

Bolivian weather: a complex made simple by its fact; does not
want, as me, to be noticed, is a wrap neither hot nor cold,

requires minor adjustments: the high sun beautiful, equatorial
— the breeze exactly at

the point I need it — the summer rain   in the city of La Paz.

            •

we drive
to Sorata

by jeep, up to the Alto Plano, through slums to the more
pastoral. Bolivia is ground, brown to green, each inch an
agricultural possibility; then to brown again, dots of rocks — the
impossible land scape of mountain / moraine that yields at the lip
of the descent into the Andes valleys huge / open descending
bowls of an ascending geometry (farms / measured hectares of
hand carved earth / greens to the upper glacial /   margins.

Sorata

The Oasis.   resort of sorts not quite right but as an unfinished
plan out of synch (homemade signs "Camping" "Baño"
"Restaurante"— North American style / campground being
eaten by the flood. we mud it to town, the square, the church,
the internet, the international telefono — markets, tiendas,
cafes, the *holas, buenos dias* — Spanish greetings as
pattern become repetition.   the familiar / to the ease of easier
maneuvers: "habitation con baño? con ducha?" I ask.   bold
enough to fuck up.   let your guard down: think, *paradise is a
complex*

convergence:

its opposite: 2 sides with guns who shoot it out (La Paz Policia
versus Bolivian Army / 30 dead

or
the guy in Sucre at the moment I thought, <u>*this*</u> *is paradise*, tells us

his pocket slit, wallet taken, then dropped in the fight. welcome
to . . .

any world we know is impending: *adjust*, continue through
cobbled streets — think, the simultaneous & coincident: *good
and evil* — every moment holding
inherent threat / possibility

•

Bolivia,   Bolivia

•

— in the weight of *every thing*, not merely noticed, but *taken in*:
carnival sounds, the wobbly drums, all combos of Bolivian
colour (reds, ochres, the pastel wash, whitewashed brick beneath
the canopies of tin — Bolivia *crumbling* in the repeated 4 bar
brass Bolivian riffs in the dance & human shuffle of its own
celebration.

•

JOURNAL: *Feb 13: leave Sorata. Ricardo's jeep up to Achicachi.
Harris says: a shithole! La Paz in riot — police vs army (issues
of income tax?) total 30 dead — looting / bank machines
smashed / fires etc. conflict also in Cusco? Potosi? — threat of
general strike? my real sense of fear in this context. <u>also</u> of coca
farmers, Campesinos blocking roads. no taxi or bus to take us
safe & out. store packs with Juan at hotel. Viv to walk out or
hire bike to road blocks, see what's up. Jesus! we walk to edge of
town. gringos. pure fear. Joy says take an Ativan. want beer / to
go home. say to John this is not my fucking idea of fun, I'd
fucking go home this min. if I cld. mouth dry. word is that cars
coming thru. get a taxi (Alfredo? despite rumors of blockades
drives us to ferry & from there take microbus to Copacabana.*

116

guy on bus (hidalgo? an engineer fills Viv in on La Paz. he left
this a.m. & walked thru road blocks 30 km — worried. advised
us to keep going into Peru

•

get to
Cocacabana: through hills / down to Lake Titicaca — the intense
sun, the intense blue, the Mediterranean / Bolivia. a "beautiful
setting". "good to see tourists" I write, "sense of safety here."

thinking of La Paz, write: *sense of no control or way out if*
trouble comes yr way. side note: cant sleep properly. (altitude?
drink coca tea / rain temp: perfect for me.

the brain works its spectrums and doubles — from weight of self
importance, to / sense of *I don't care*

(Bolivian farmers cling to the sliding hill, become earth
themselves, a move of colour in slow stooped moves to plant —

•

JOURNAL: *Feb 14th: never any sense of discomfort in "weather*
" — sun / hi altitude.   (7.7 Bolivianos = 1$US).   at hotel
120 B's (bfast included). lunch very cheap 6 B's – & hike up
behind town to ancient cave site — & on down valley & up
to Inca drawings — ☐ ☐ ☐ series of squares (red). hard to
see point / meaning. local farmer describes / "meaning" in
Spanish / Incan history etc. give his kid a candy, a pen & a few
pages from notebook. beautiful sun / clear — back to highway
(note old air strip) warm 3:30 - flag taxi, 2B each and back to
Copa (meet Dutch travelers, Hendrick and Emilie at bar "Ricks
Place" — have beer — supper). to bed. sleep a problem. wake up
at 12. cant get back to sleep — altitude? feel pretty good during
the day.

who in their heads, think what? is it
to diminish fear with the familiar, the repeat of daily routine
to be one's self while about you

the poor /

the dark Bolivian stars, on the all night Flota from Potosi
to La Paz?

.

JOURNAL: *Feb 15: up at 6:00. beautiful sky / boats on lake. cld
see lights of Puno across. electric shower luke warm / catch boat
"Titanic" at 8:30 to Isla del Sol (2½ hrs) <u>slow</u> along coast thru
2 narrow channels. land at Cha'llapampa & go on to Inca town
thru old lady's yard: <u>vamoose! vamoose!</u> irritated. she waves
us on to the Inca ruin. cant understand the guide's narrative
— an explanation of Inca mythology. sense he didn't know
what he was talking abt. lady guide finishes talk. no baño. piss
behind ruins and hike on up the Inca ridge. eat lunch at 1:00.
Viv makes tomato/onion sandwich. excellent — & then on
walking / talking w/ John abt college politics, writing, pensions
— no diff than we've ever talked —*

.

sun & weather: the Isla del Sol

JOURNAL: *Feb 16: Viv takes pic. me w / Llama (spits!). kids on
trail selling rocks (<u>senior, Inca! Inca!</u> Viv barters. I buy one for
1B — give kid another .50 B get another rock! these are the only
rocks I'll keep, I think — eyeball vista thinking I'll never forget
this, but probably will — <u>the contours, colours smells, textures</u>:
no real way to document the detail. "description" of "3rd
world?" (is there worse ahead. what world's next?*

— walk rocky Inca path

*to top of town / no trail markers. perdido! "lost" & ask 2
locals direction. w/ no words for "boat", "water" etc. tho I
remember the boat is called "Titanic". I ask, "donde Titanic?
Titanic?" question doesn't register. instead guy shows me his
hat / says "Llama! Llama!"*

in Bolivia detail is reality.
Peru is motive

JOURNAL: *Feb 17 Monday: Lv Copa for Puno thru Kasani.
micro bus to border — 2 border checks – no problems — Puno
— a shithole!, John says / sheds, shacks — taxis, bike taxis,
stink of diesel & burnt out motors, Lake Titicaca — green
polluted ring — hot: walk into town w/ packs — winded
— ask directions to plaza — & head up. main street — banks,
restaurants — mid class mixed w/ tourists, police, shoe shine
boys, beggars, locals etc.*

— swarmed by shoe shine boys. two on
each boot, laces removed. my pack Viv thinks is next.

in Peru
what's learned, a pattern: one price to begin, a higher price to
end.   the tactic: hound tourists
until
they give in / or be as the well dressed gringo on Isla del Sol
waving
them off: *get away! get away!*

JOURNAL: *Feb 19 head into Andes. beautiful verdant hills (fertile) w/ Andes behind — hours of travel thru small villages. lots of food / vendors on buses — corn, pop, cups of red (jello? etc. nb. woman hacking turkey out of backpack. note: — 2 police checks for "contraband". John out to watch packs. no real sense of what they're looking for. <u>scary</u>. a routine*

Juliaca: incredible mix / people — but <u>all</u> poor. dirt, dust, garbage, stink, woman sweeping garbage to garbage. no hope. this is <u>total</u> poverty / stink. bus winds thru mud streets / vendors markets etc. sense of no one working unless waiting is the work — what's the economy?

these — stretches, mountains undulations rhythms and
   lines / potholes

     — bus without shocks

to Cusco Peru

   •

old voices leave me / sentiments and measures replaced —

emptied

Cusco: Inca city   / replaced: colonial Spanish impositions, inquisitions and worse. piece it together how? Bolivar, Pizarro
   — names of streets, statues, heroes / villains

South America.

the perfect fit of Inca stones form Cusco's lower foundation
— the rest dismantled, replaced with curly Spanish stone &
iron /   churches — evidence of commerce and
robbery

museums / Inca pieces — Spanish colonial remnant and artifact how to know   or fit anywhere

•

in Cusco: hawkers, the plaza ringed, territory staked, tourists
stalked / menus thrust to the face: "my friend, you eat here!"

"tomorrow"

"tomorrow! tomorrow! maybe next year!"

equivalent of *fuck you.*

or / the lady with the painted gourd hitting it over and over: "no
ceramico! no ceramico!" a block later you give in — 10 Soles

these measures of someone's hell / money
strapped to your balls

•

drink at bar, *Norton's Rat* (Jeff, American ex pat: "muggers
strangle you to point of death — leave you
stripped . . . lived in Juliaca. rent 35 US a month / my
neighbor / priest. some kind of
hassle . . .
they blew his house up"

•

buy ripped off package to Machu
Pichu

$100 US

admit to thin identity of being

Machu Pichu / no urgency to reach Incan / Mecca.   the slow train
makes its way / along Urabamba — a rush of mud — impatient
turbulence / a gush to the Amazon: birds / trees — more
  "tropical"

— mountains

"mystical".   mist circling /   greens / grays — the vertical cliffs
of

Machu Pichu

photo of me in spot where Al Purdy stood
— the sugar loaf mountain Earle Birney climbed behind me.

the tour: I cling to the rocks with vertigo & savor the guide's
narration:

see the Inca world: sun dial damaged in beer ad shoot! see the
condor's shape and wings! / a cosmology / teleology: everything, I
think, is fortress / is enemy.

"beautiful"

•

JOURNAL: *Feb 21: Cusco: tourism hustle at high pitch and
annoying. Bolivia starts to look much better — less tourist hype.
cheaper. lv Cusco. get large bus (pink style flotta), back thru
Andes high valleys, back thru Juliaca / Puno — Copacabana
— back to La Paz.*

in these routes retraced, know more — *miles & patterns* — &
know less / the political configurations, history — that nothing
quite works yet.

.

La Paz in the words
of the local, is *tranquilo / normal*

Bolivianos dolled out in eye of smiling guys with guns.

quick clouds & rain. revolution & coup — *Bolivia*

.

we walk La Paz again. plaza shot up. coffee / cheesecake at
Alexander's. desayuno at
Dumbos.

JOURNAL: *Feb 23 here, amazed at the mix: a middle class,
indigenous, plump ladies in mushroom dresses, bowler
hats / Hidalgos, army / police — private cops in blue
snowmobile suits / shoe shine boys w / masks (Viv heard that
kids non-unionized wear masks to hide identity or to protect
vs fumes? the hills of mud abt to slide — downtown a kind of
little New York / the morning explosion of activity, off the main,
treed streets embassies, apts, American style restaurants / the
Thelonious Jazz Club — big band, w / Indians, Spaniards
led by Dane, Anders Andersen on tenor — read tough jazz
charts / swing and improvise.*

*downtown La Paz / Viv w/ helpful Hidalgos at broken bank
machine. / amused guy w/ machine gun comes over, curious.
Bolivian toddler grasps my hand — choked up by little kid's
curiosity, trust, innocence / vs what we know and learn as
opposites.*

.

fly to Sucre

*JOURNAL: Feb 26 — landscape below, mountains — smears
of red / green, — rivers — brown / wide. land. take taxi to
town. Sucre: 1st impression: old, colonial, clean — a change
from usual slums of Bolivian city outskirts. "paradise" of
sorts (weather, architecture & sense of "good place to be". at
point of thinking this, French Canadian guy tells us abt being
robbed / scammed earlier in the day. guy is diverted while robber
slits his pocket w/ razor blade.*

*great sleep! no altitude probs here so far. — Saturday: walk w/
packs & bags. get taxi for 90 B's — 3 hrs climb thru countryside*

to Potosi

•

what gets identified the moment you sense identification lost
as your life on the roads to Potosi — John shaking
the driver awake. I'm under a bag / coming to the literal heights
  & end

of Bolivia

(head clear / a few words /   my sense of transgression

to
Po to si   high in the silver
Andes — colour change / weather change — cold (bleak,   clouds
& chill in wind

walk on the bones of six million worked to death / though no
graves to mark them (blacks from Amazon / kids from anywhere

mid 1500's all the world's silver   Bolivian coins shipped out
to Spain

from Potosi's mountain — Cerro Rico / the mint

    •

at the la Hostal Compaña de Jesus — I write, "a bit under
construction". Joy says, "a rathole" — 40 B's a night / toss cold
in my sleepless nights, write: "the place cold. bombed by globos.
everyone WET"

"every 30 seconds need a big breath"

    •

in fragments of fragmented place what souvenir contains it / or
thought of heart & mind yield its sense & meaning?

the bus ride from Potosi to La Paz is dark, a backroad
bumpy / slow —a metaphor, but of what?
when I wake: "no crying babies. *everyone* asleep." I look &
think — are the stars in the Bolivian sky, cold? dark? in the bleak
& cold

"a wonderful sense
of moving"

sense the weight place takes.   *human.*

Bolivia   Bolivia

    •

       leaving
/ its memory   ahead of me

    •

La Paz: the morning / leaving: keep trying / tying pieces — string

the wordless image of the imagination — a defiance to the
humble recognition of any attempt

we tie up bags with string. get taxi in pre dawn — commingle /
in happy sense to leave / no thought of coming back / no
memory yet in the immediate detail of the climb up
to Alto Plano to airport & single thought of home.

La Paz doesn't twinkle behind: it exists; the farmers
coming in (ancient cycles & routines

produce & coca leaves
— last chance for airport souvenirs: I buy 2 beers (Pilsen &
   Pacena)

jet out & down / the Andes, high arc & down to the coast &
   Lima Peru
think of the day coming in —
same steward (lousy coffee / Nescafé?

land in the heat of Lima / grey   thin clouded coast. sun breaks
   through

with 15 hours to kill.

•

write: *don't have any portents about lima /*

hot

take taxi downtown — miles of incredible poverty / thru
slums to main plaza — the Peruvian tourist hustle — square
looks ok — incredible colonial structures — changing of the
guards / police

walk toward the church /
over the boiling / mudshit Rio Rimac

to the meaning of one's big moment
between life and death —

mugged

on a corner   in Lima Peru.

                •

(robber grabs purse. flash of red. no face / body — Joy screaming
my name — clutches purse to chest, then flipped / back to the
ground dragged in / along street. guy <u>won't</u> let go. no thinking.
the pure action of all bodies adrenalized response. seconds?
I yell <u>you cocksucker!</u> raise travel book "Peru" above my
head & bring it down full force to guy's head. Joy released. I
fall full force, dead weight to ground. wrists hit first. elbow,
legs — physical terror. violence. desperations. get up yell to
crowd — <u>get away you fuckers!</u> Joy ok — bruised. my wrists
hurt elbow bleeding long scratch on leg. duck into 1st safe
looking restaurant. drink 2 beers. in shock — get safe taxi out.
remember sympathetic waiter in Spanish sd:

            — in life there is good, there is bad.

            •

as simple demonstration of anyone's care,

pilot asks, *how are you tonight, sir?*

I'm bleeding

are you emotionally ok?   soon — I'll have you 35,000 feet
and home

•

impossible /

presumption of conclusions — a habit of the world now broken

fucked up by mugging / choked by what we come to know

that the eye, is also the mind, & contains it as large as it was

•

maps and places, muds and shapes   & colours
of a peopled earth — poignancy's, complexities of mind
and place —
                    Bolivia /   Peru

Sixty

for Ken Belford
and the memory of
Robert Creeley

sixty:

 no sense
of beginning — beginning sense of ends

thinking —

   the in between

         memory gardens,

   — a whole   unfinished

   •

45 years ago in spring
green, fecund on my way.
— the moment said, *this is /*
the moment's moment:

— as first site
of the milky breast in moonlight — river, trees — at the dead end
   making out

     to pleasure / to suspension / to being

   •

my mother   on the porch, smoking — held a Melmac cup,
was beauty to me

   — *the self emerging   is known and given*

•

I had no words
no answer
I was held *in* by meanies & punished all the more. I stopped
speaking   and refused Latin blackboard drills

•

in
defeat   I thought I saw   a way

　　　　　— to embrace

the now   surpass
explanation / rules

•

I stare out, the ticking clock.   blinds part
drawn, rippled breeze in trees — script / scriven
　　contents of a given you cannot describe —

•

I'm drawn by a blank sensation

•

you have a very full life —

•

as any other measure as that caught in what it
thought — to say   what?

life un
folding folds the equation
it attempts

the' older   I get

·

he's not afraid of anything

·

death —
say it.   these days.   life
is its condition elaborated in the face /   *nothingness in space*

·

no place *but context* (sinewed time & body   its memory —
the house on 15th I lived in gone.   I drive on

·

my suspended head scary / revolves. I'm a
low number on a scale. the here & now of non resolve a
constant I now see? neutral blurs & shapes

·

& what thought
    as fragment is pieces: *to enter world / to leave the earth*

I sense now   the surfaces — a commingling wish to be no one
yet not separate from what seen

otherwise:

the corporate picture — we are small as a bug in / millennial
    ruins —
        the last dash —
for ... energy transformed

    •

I fear what dark reveals, yet this
revelry
        of light. *morning.* some regret. *failure no longer
matters* as time crunches to its future diminished

    •

the transition *is* happiness — illusions gone / to *faith*

— a zeroed consciousness less faked — wisps ...

out of breath father pissing   in a parking lot: — an
old man

I do what I want.

    •

in Grade 1 over the Plasticene forest I saw the trees —
rustled leaves quiet in my anxious break when space of mind
sees space

    •

time not memory but dream. *places.*   dark
purples streaked low and east 50
years ago, last night or night before —

    •

disappearance is weightless (all that was or is to a narrowed
horizon — the surprise of self enacted to know no more
   need to its surprise

    •

yet thought up the canyon — *love increased by threat*
of its loss — itself a season, its intensity increased by sense
of diminished time. mottled colour & leaves. the simplest /
most intense —

sensed myself
— a laconic embodiment   neutral
in the neutral air. I sensed — words stripped, flesh of season /
   reasons gone.   what words?

    •

at sixty

    ... a presence

that resembles nothing but itself —

        by the condition of its source

         to bear its thought

Prince George Core

for Sharon Thesen

city, mind — body.

the mind disintegrates. the body   now a shell

"everything must go".   so the shell is left — its last punch
through the wall — broken

windows

empty   *for lease /*

                    for sale

the city

          core /

Saturday Jan. 12: up 3rd, sense this: *not followed* but what's
ahead / to the thrift store, my fear: I cannot easily pass through

                    / crack heads /

desperate predation & no sense of *what*
they could ever care

: the city as body — began, arked, disintegrated. garbage strewn,
lumps of clothes / single shoes / bags of needles / thrift store
moved or bankrupt though the goods they sold were free

to my right, natives clumped, stoned and grinning, once
dispossessed, to be dispossessed again / not mingling, but
clumped by the abandoned Food Teller doorway / wait for crack,
booze and heroin

what it is, *is*. cruel that body and mind sense their own demise.
the city is organ. it sees itself. disintegrated. its body and mind
its own demise

turning left, sense *nothings left*. "closed / staff shortage"

give shake of head,

fucked / without a voice.

the heart did not break / became homeless: we stood boneless in
a heap / stunned then drunk, *not seen as the map*, the city, the
larger world — emptied of resource. no recourse to the map that
once led / to the wilderness back to the path it once was. in this
heap, stolen bikes through snow — the grinning homeless lad
either in legitimacy says *hello sir* — the friendly light of human
greeting or as sardonic gesture: *fuck you.*

garbage, demise — butts, puke, sand / gravel, the snowy streets.
slush to mud by the Ramada / *everywhere* — the opera as
backdrop, the screeching of a high human voice to keep these
humans away — bums on George. what wealth / squeezed,
burned, horded as the world went / everywhere else but here.
so as I, city at last with out illusion or dream or grandeur — or
friendly face / sincerity — is it the care of David Petrescu I miss
who saw the pleasures and treasures of the dump, the beer as
source for possibility, the Cottonwood flood, a sign to move.
there is no choice when of a place it is the place you'll be

metaphors of recognition / value of what is seen, exposed. the
body, raw, open, sexy in its arc, ugly in demise, aging to know
body and soul are *one*. the mind disintegrates / is the heap of
clothes, dumped as the he / she walked out into snow & cold, no
light ahead on the dark road beyond

here. decay, cliché — in the shit of the city / of city fathers, I
look for . . . *vision care. mind care. heart care. body care* — all
that's lost but our cheery thought / foolish reminiscence to
ask / names of all gone in the toxicity of age itself   not knowing
how to turn. John Harris would ask for a vision, the alternate. I
can't find the grammar machine — make no proposal /

give thanks /

grumble in the arc and demise. sense it always here, *that*
beginning illusion. I so lost in whatever task sought — sense
of work, to do good & in the face of a force sent out to beat it,
but that *that* gave resolve and strength — my endurance in the

face of such shallow delights they sought by removing what little delight we had. many will not see:

the imported force, their source unknown, the conspiracy, piracy of those in charge

a world is made — of mud / become bone, sinewed road / a habitat of beauty, raw rivers to meet. the confluent / myth / abundance — dance of possibility — imagined before global demand became a line / or time, split & frayed by industrial demand no locals could fight or resist, driven to slick and simple rhetoric — that abundance as goal became its own & pure objective goal. *the trees.* paradise ahead like history

swaths / rectangles / some messy cuts in the contours I saw in 69. sometimes sense, *much still left.* the mind disintegrates, the body arches & all the more such strength to require faith, some sense of decency in whatever mistake was made.   I build a fire, I see it — call it — / the aging body drawn by last wish, not to think: *what's deserved / not deserved.* the fire burns. regret, all not done / what done gone

the old   city /   core

disintegrates — simultaneously evolves / to malls / outsourced plenitude — the perpetual motion of returned goods — an isolation once sensed defines us being here without

when I saw the dark — became pulp myself / in the glimmer of the dark winter snow

Joy says *let it go* — as if some other force must be known / defeat the past & open an opening brief to future light: *you decide*

in the body's arc / demise —

the mind as habitat. city gone, overtaken — divided: those who enter the bank / those who wait — beg spare change. slush & snow, the diesel air — sense of a shitkick to the soul. some *thing* battered in front of us.   the body disintegrates. the mind some final habitat

the city   hates itself

peeled back / no false surface, in the surfeit — wealth can falsely bring

3rd & George. no children on these streets, is true, yet so large this recognition / simple eyes open to what is seen: *no children on these streets*

old days? maybe nothing's changed — no sense of going on / to question the ebb and flow of social energies that the biggest thing cannot be seen: the drivers in the growing economies / talking heads / coughed slogans / toxic cliché and denial. what was I going to say given this window of opportunity in the 24/7/365 — this thinking a complex mask, or heard as specious airy thought? — no one expelled from paradise *is irony*

in the 30 below. I'm on the streets again — list the close-outs, pawn shops belly-up, though cheer the mainstays — the tenacious: Morrisons, Prudentes, Moffats, McGinnis — the German bakers / the shops on 4th — outsourced to College Heights, Hwy 16, box store clerks mumbling *have a nice day*

what is left. brooding, landscapes / ravaged. trees – in many places gone. logging. bugs. stock piles — sense of world fast tracked for the last grab / *this is eco nomics*

sun, bright to my left, south rays intensified.   35 below.   chill factor. the tenacious north

what we become

/ this sense of home / the desire to leave
— time and *life, a river* (eddies, swirls / floods /   the digital earth

Notes

Bolivia / Peru

Bolivia / Peru is a chronological assemblage of journal notes, thoughts, splices, poems, questions & reflections inspired by a 5-week trip to South America.

I think we're moving into a new & necessary time for poetry: the poem has to resemble the nature of the various & fractured realities it addresses without presumption, and be wary even of the emotions & thoughts & forms & devices that promote it.

In *Bolivia / Peru* I've had to struggle with sentimentalities, notions & slants from a North American perspective that do not work or address the larger task of what I think the poem must reveal. In South America I was in a complex without knowing the histopoliticosocio, and therefore entered naked / naive to its experience — perhaps the only way to risk any world's range of pleasures / dangers, and in this weight to thankfully and humbly survive it — to know a little more.

In the Bolivian and Peruvian countryside houses and huts are built with bricks of mud that slowly dissolve in the weather. In this way I want the poem to stand, be habitable, and yet show dissolving forces. My attempt to impose an architecture, however crude, is part of the struggle and pleasure of the writing.

The journal notes were written in Bolivia & Peru from Feb 7 to Mar 11, 2003. Journal entries that appear in the text — the sections in italics — are transcribed as originally jotted.

Text assemblage: April–July 2003 in Prince George / Tumbler Ridge, B.C.

Prince George Core

The descriptions / images in this poem, for the most part, are a result of walks from the Millar Addition to and through the Prince George downtown city core — its centre at 3rd and George.

The Food Teller is an abandoned restaurant on the corner of 5th and George, across from the Ramada Hotel. It is a street of bars, a decaying cabaret, drop-in centres, a thrift store, a second-hand book store, a cold beer and wine store, etc. Opera blasts daily from the Ramada, presumably as an aural abrasive to drive away lingerers, dope dealers, hookers, transients, etc.

David Petrescu was a friend who died too young, but taught me the pleasures of the downtown in earlier days (buns and meatballs from the German bakery, beers at the old Astoria and the Canada hotels) — and developed my eye for eccentric thrift store junk.

Cottonwood Island at the confluence of the Nechako and Fraser rivers has been flooded many times over the years, and eventually forced the inhabitants of the Island Cache to move to higher ground in the 70's. Houses and shacks were abandoned and later bulldozed. The 2008 ice jam / flood, the worst in 50 years, backed up the Nechako 26 km and into the suburbs.

The Moffat, Morrison, Prudente, and McGinnis families, among several others, are longtime independent store owners in the downtown core. They stay and survive despite the heavy competition from the box stores and malls that have killed much of their business.

John Harris is a friend and writer with an intellect of large proportions who inspires much of what I have come to see and believe about place, politics, and literature.

Joy, my wife — practical, impatient & laconic who gives clear-headed advice in disturbing contexts. When I didn't have a title she said: *you're writing about the core.*

the city hates itself — is a line from my friend and colleague Anna Djuric.

Prince George is peeled back — a line of observation from the poet Lissa Wolsak.

life is like a river is a line from Robert Creeley's poem "A Full Cup" in his last book, *On Earth.*

Acknowledgment of publications where sections of *In the Millennium* first appeared

JOURNAL PUBLICATIONS
The Capilano Review
West Coast Line
Textual Studies in Canada

ONLINE JOURNALS
It's Still Winter: A Journal of Contemporary Canadian Poetry and Poetics. http://quarles.unbc.ca/winter.
Philly Talks #18: C.S. Giscombe and Barry McKinnon. Responses by Wade Compton, George Elliot Clarke, & Giovanni Singleton, Feb 2001. http://philly talks.org/library.

ANTHOLOGIES
Baird, Jean, David McFadden and George Stanley. Eds. *71(+) for GB: An Anthology for George Bowering on the Occasion of His 70th Birthday*. Toronto: Coach House Press, 2005.
Atwood, Margaret. *The New Oxford Book of Canadian Verse*. Toronto: Oxford, 1978.
Hui, Zhu. *Selected Canadian Lyrics*. Sichuan, China: Sichuan University Press, 1995.

CHAPBOOKS
Two from In the Millennium [*Prince George (Part 1)* and *Sixty*]. Toronto: Bookthug, 2006.
Boliva / Peru. Prince George: Gorse Press, 2004. Winner of the bp Nichol Chapbook Award for the best poetry chapbook published in English, 2004.

Surety Disappears. Prince George: Gorse Press. Runner-up for the bp Nichol Chapbook Award in 2008.

Head Out: A Letter. Essay. Poem. to Cecil Giscombe. Prince George: Gorse Press, 2007.

The following sections were printed at various times by Gorse Press in limited editions for private distribution: *In the Millennium*, *A Walk*, *Sex at 52*, *An Unfinished Theology*, *It Can't Be Said*, *Joy (An Epithalamium)*, *Bastard File*, *Transliteration*, and *Prince George Core*.

Grateful thanks to the BC Arts Council for a writing grant.

All quotes and poems by Cecil Giscombe appear with the kind permission from Dalkey Archive Press, copyright 2007, C.S. Giscombe.

Other New Star poetry titles

Annharte
  Exercises In Lip Pointing (2003)

Stephen Collis
  Mine (2001)
  Anarchive (2005)

Peter Culley
  Hammertown (2003)
  The Age of Briggs & Stratton (2008)

Maxine Gadd
  Backup To Babylon (2006)
  Subway Under Byzantium (2008)

Andrew Klobucar & Michael Barnholden, eds.
  *Writing Class: The Kootenay School Of Writing
  Anthology* (1999)

Justin Lukyn
  Henry Pepper (2008)

Donato Mancini
  Ligatures (2005)
  Æthel (2007)

Roy Miki
  There (2006)

Lisa Robertson
  Debbie: An Epic (1997)
  XEclogue (1999)
  The Weather (2001)

Jordan Scott
  Silt (2005)

George Stanley
  Gentle Northern Summer (1995)
  At Andy's (2000)
  Vancouver: A Poem (2008)

Simon Thompson
  Why Does It Feel So Late? (2009)

In the Millennium presents the major work of the last decade from Barry McKinnon. The poems, with their combination of verse lines and prose passages, their jumps, gaps, and hesitations, meticulously register the subject's response to his environment: to human processes, conditions and places; to love, sex, death, the insecurities and pressures of the inner and outer world.

'The Millennium *poems are jagged the way an accompaniment is when heard on its own, and brilliant. Barry is one of the very best poets in this country, always will be.'* — **Sharon Thesen**

'*In his pursuit to find what is essentially "ours", Barry has become the necessary poet. He writes out of critical necessity, and not for literary affect. He wants the real goods. That's what you get when you read his poems.'* — **David Phillips**

Barry McKinnon lives in Prince George. He is the author of eight poetry books, including *Pulp Log*, which won the Dorothy Livesay Poetry Prize in 1992, and *The the*, a finalist for the Governor-General's Award in 1982.

Poetry

A New Star book
Cover design: Clint Hutzulak/Mutasis.com
Cover photograph by Joy McKinnon
Printed on recycled paper
Printed and bound in Canada

ISBN 978-1-55420-047-4

9 781554 200474